# Mr. Buffer's SAT/ACT
## ScoreMax Program

# SAT/ACT Reading/Writing Workbook

*A great tool to help you master the SAT/ACT Reading & Writing sections and to understand the great value of learning concepts fundamentally*

*Prepared for you by Mr. Justin Buffer, MSE, Founder, Owner, and Educational Director, of the Cambridge Learning Center of New Jersey, located in North Brunswick, NJ, one of the tri-state's premiere learning centers.*

# 2018CombVers V1

JMB Publishing
Academic and Personal Growth

is publication may be reproduced, stored in a retrieval system, or transmitted in any form or by any means electronic, mechanical, photocopying, recording or otherwise without the prior permission of the publisher.   Permission is hereby granted for students to make copies for homework, study, and test preparatory © COPYRIGHT JMB PUBLISHING AND MR. JUSTIN BUFFER, FOUNDER, OWNER, AND DIRECTOR, CAMBRIDGE LEARNING CENTER OF NJ,  NORTH BRUNSWICK, NJ, 2016

ISBN # **978-1539588320**


**PUBLICATION DATE:   MARCH 1, 2018**

## IMPORTANT WEBSITES FOR YOU TO KNOW ABOUT

## 1) Cambridge Student Practice Website

### www.cambridgenjstudents.com

This site is where you will sign up for your online vocabulary test and where you will find many practice problems to do.

## 2)  College Board Website

### www.collegeboard.org

This site is where you will go sign up for you SAT, as well as retrieve your scores and where you will eventually go to send your scores to the colleges you apply to.

## 3) **ACT Website**

www.act.org

This site is where you will go sign up for you ACT, as well as retrieve your scores and where you will eventually go to send your scores to the colleges you apply to.

## Q & A With Mr. Buffer on the Writing Sections of the SAT and ACT

Mr. Justin Buffer, MSE, - *Mr. Buffer, a New Jersey Licensed K-12 Teacher, is the Founder, Owner/Creator, and Director of the Cambridge Learning Center of New Jersey. He has a Masters Degree in Educational Theory and Practice & Educational Psychology and has designed all of Cambridge's programs and curriculum himself. He also owns JMB Publishing, Cambridge Learning Center's own publishing company and attended the Rutgers Graduate School of Education. He is an author and contributed to the "Seven Points of Impact" book, published by LFK Publishing ®, writing a chapter on effective pedagogy. He*

*is also a College Planner, Personal Development/Life Coach, and Motivational Speaker.*

**The following interview was done with Mr. Buffer by a professional interviewer and his responses are transcribed below. Your teacher will read through his answers with you prior to going over the SAT and ACT Writing sections, as well as Mr. Buffer's Signature Grammar Excellence Program. ® ©**

*****************************************

<u>1)</u>  **Question for Mr. Buffer: Mr. Buffer, what is the underlying purpose of your SAT/ACT Grammar Excellence Plan?**

    **Answer from Mr. Buffer:** The underlying purpose of this section is to provide a strong foundational basis for the SAT and ACT Writing Sections. One key thing that we do here at Cambridge is teaching at a fundamental level. It is a core part of my pedagogical philosophy. My experience shows me that if students are only or mostly taught test-taking strategies without really deeply understanding the fundamentals of the grammatical and writing concepts, they will not succeed as much as they will if they know the vernacular of standard written English clearly, as well as all aspects of core Writing Fundamentals. So, for example, let's just say a student gets three questions wrong in the SAT Language/Writing section about Unity and

Coherence. If a teacher was to teach him or her tricks and strategies about how to get the right answer , instead of really helping the student understand Unity and Coherence as principles in and of themselves separate from the SAT and ACT, what I know from my research and my work here is that they will not be as successful.

It doesn't mean they won't get one or two more questions correct by getting to know the test better and learning strategies and tricks; such things have a role to play for sure. But they will be much more successful and consistently successful for the long-term if they understand them at a foundational level. As a teacher, even as a classroom teacher, I've always believed in beginning your teaching at a foundational level and working your way up, and this is the philosophical underpinning embedded into the SAT/ACT Grammar Excellence program I created.

# The New York Times

## A GREAT TOOL TO HELP YOU ENRICH YOUR READING SKILLS AND PERFORM BETTER ON THE SAT/ACT

*1) To help you with your reading comprehension, breadth of knowledge, and exposure to sophisticated levels of writing, as well as different writing styles, **you should make a goal each week to read a minimum of 4 full editorials from the New York Times Opinion Page or articles from any other section of the New York Times.***

*2) Circle any vocabulary words you don't know **and define them in the Vocabulary Section of this workbook.***

## The websites to find the articles and editorials are:

### www.nytimes.com

### www.nytimes.com/opinion

\*\*\*\*\*\*\*\*\*\*\*\*\*\*\*\*\*\*\*\*\*\*

# S-503: MR. BUFFER'S  WEEKLY

# SAT STUDY PLAN AND  BEST PRACTICES FOR YOUR OPTIMAL SCORE: UPDATED 8/19/16

1)     Study your SAT flashcards daily for all areas- Reading, Writing, and Math.  Try to average 40 new cards per week, and make this process cumulative.  Also, make sure you are taking *Mr. Buffer's Online SAT Vocabulary Test* bi-weekly as this will greatly help you with the Critical Reading section of the test.

*2)*     Aim to review your mistakes from in-class and from your previously checked homework from all SAT/ACT Subject Areas (Math, Reading, and Writing). You should be taking notes during your sessions and studying them at home. This is how most of your time should be spent.  ***Before taking practice test after practice test, and asking to take test after test, you should focus on studying.***  What I (Mr. Buffer) have always told students is that *"You don't test your way to success.  You study your way to success." **This should be done for 1.5 hours per day minimum, but you should aim for more.***

3)     Come to class ready to ask questions to your teachers, and you can also ask Mr. Buffer any questions you have about SAT prep.   You can also see or make an appointment with Mr. Buffer (Cambridge Founder and Owner) at any time

about questions related to college choice.  Just make an
appointment with the front desk.

4)    We will automatically book you for a progress test every 24
      hours of SAT Tutoring.   Make sure you are checking your
      e-mail for these notifications; you can also ask at the front
      desk for your testing schedule.   If you cannot come in for
      your test, it will be your job to contact us to reschedule.

5)    Your homework will mostly be supplemental work.  You do
      not have to time yourself for this.  This is your time to refine
      your skills.

**6) Practice tests at home:** Sometimes for homework, you can time
yourself and take a practice test, but this is separate from your
Cambridge homework, but make sure someone else times you.
You should make things as close to real testing conditions as
possible.

7)  Keep yourself motivated by trying to get a little better each day,
not expecting huge leaps in one day or one
week.   Success is built one moment at a time!
We are here to help you succeed!

\* \* \* \* \* \* \* \* \* \* \* \* \* \* \* \* \* \*

# SA-504: MR. BUFFER'S  WEEKLY

# ACT STUDY PLAN AND  BEST PRACTICES FOR YOUR OPTIMAL SCORE

1) Study your ACT flashcards daily *for all areas- Reading, Writing, Math, and Science.* Try to average 30-40 new cards per week, and make this process cumulative. Also, make sure you are taking *Mr. Buffer's Online SAT/ACT Vocabulary Test* bi-weekly as this will greatly help you with the Reading section of the test, and help make sure your vocabulary is strong to be integrated into your ACT Essay.

*2)* Aim to review your mistakes from in-class and from your previously checked homework from all ACT Subject Areas (Math, Reading, Science, and Writing). You should be taking notes during your sessions and studying them at home. This is how most of your time should be spent. *Before taking practice test after practice test, and/or asking to take test after test, you should focus on studying.* What I (Mr. Buffer) have always told students is that *"You don't test your way to success. You study your way to success." This should be done for 1.5 hours per day minimum, but you should aim for more.*

3) Come to class ready to ask questions to your teachers, and you can also ask Mr. Buffer any questions you have about ACT prep. You can also see or make an appointment with Mr. Buffer (Cambridge Founder and Owner) at any time about questions related to college choice. Just make an appointment with the front desk

4) We will automatically book you for a progress test every 24 hours of ACT Tutoring. You can also ask at the front desk for your testing schedule. If you cannot come in for your test, it will be your job to contact us to reschedule.

5) Study all of your other SA Sheets (These are for ACT). These will help you maximally prepare for the ACT.

6) Be regularly aware of your major areas for growth and make sure your Live Work Journal is always being signed.

7) You will do a lot of ACT problems for homework. Make sure that you are jotting down notes you have to bring in with your teachers.

8) Here is what a typical day can look like for ACT studying:

A) 40-65 Minutes: Homework ACT Problems (Assigned)
B) 40-65 Minutes:  Review and Study previous mistakes, flashcards (See procedure and details above), and write down questions  I have to bring into class.

9) Your homework will mostly be supplemental work.  You do not have to time yourself for this.  This is your time to refine your skills.

10) **Practice tests at home:** Sometimes for homework you can time yourself and take a practice test, but this is separate from your Cambridge homework, but make sure someone else times you when you do.  You should make things as close to real testing conditions as possible.

**11)**     Keep yourself motivated by trying to get a little better each day, not expecting huge leaps in one day or one week.   Success is built one moment at a time! We are here to help you succeed!

# Mr. Buffer's SAT/ACT
## ScoreMax Program

### Foundational Concept#1:

### Understanding the Past Perfect Tense

\*\*\*\*\*\*\*\*\*\*\*\*\*\*\*\*\*\*\*\*\*\*\*\*\*\*\*\*\*\*\*\*\*\*

**What is the purpose of the Past-Perfect Tense?:** The purpose of the past perfect tense is to express that an event described in a sentence happened ***before*** another event that is indicated to have happened in the past. What you should know:

1) A verb must be used in the simple past in a sentence for the past perfect to then be used.

2) The past perfect always includes the word "had."

\*\*\*\*\*\*\*\*\*\*\*\*\*\*\*\*\*\*\*\*\*\*\*\*\*\*\*\*\*\*\*\*\*\*\*\*\*\*\*\*\*\*\*\*\*\*\*\*\*

\*\*\*\*\*\*\*\*\*\*\*\*\*\*\*\*\*\*\*\*\*\*\*\*\*\*\*\*\*

## Example of the correct usage of the Past Perfect:

**Example#1:**   Before Abraham Lincoln became *(Simple Past)* a successful President, he had failed (*Past Perfect*) in business and in many other areas.

In this sentence, it is indicated that Abraham Lincoln failed in business.  It is then indicated, in the same sentence, that he became President after this, thus necessitating the usage of the Past-Perfect.

**Example#2:**   Before Samantha woke up from her deep sleep *(Simple Past)*, she had been (*Past Perfect*) dreaming of her upcoming vacation to Hawaii.

In this sentence, it is indicated that Samantha had been dreaming *before* she woke up.


Can you write your own sentence using the Past Perfect tense?   Your SAT/ACT teacher will check it for you.

_____

_____

# Mr. Buffer's SAT/ACT
## ScoreMax Program

### Foundational Concept#2:  Idioms

### What is an idiom?

An idiom is a speech form or an expression of a given language that is peculiar to itself grammatically or cannot be understood from the individual meanings of its elements, as in *keep tabs on.  Idioms are a good tool to know for SAT/ACT Reading, Writing, and for general academic success.*

# SOME IMPORTANT IDIOMS

# TO KNOW FOR THE

### 1) Prefer to

**Correct Idiomatic Usage**:

*John prefers Target to Wal-Mart.*

### 2) Inconsistent with

**Correct Idiomatic Usage**:

*Sara talking behind people's backs is **inconsistent with** the person I know.*

### 3) Capable Of

**Correct Idiomatic Usage**:

*Parents whose children are in danger are **capable of** great feats of strength.*

## 4) <u>Known as (A Name)/Known to be (A quality)</u>

| Known as (A name or nickname) | *He is known to his family as Johnny.* |
|---|---|
| Known to be (A quality) | *He is known to be smart and kind.* |

## 5) Agree

| Agree or disagree with a person | I agree with Bryan. |
|---|---|
| Agree to do something | I have agreed to go on vacation to Puerto Rico. |
| Agree on (or upon) a plan of action | We both agree on the budget plan for the government. |

## 6) Distinguish (Both of these are OK)

| Distinguish from | I cannot distinguish the blue from the red in your sweater. |
|---|---|
| Distinguish between | I cannot distinguish between left and right. |

## 7) Similar/Different

| Similar  To | Kobe Bryant's style of play is *similar to* Michael's Jordan's style of play. |
|---|---|
| Different from<br>Differs from | Rubber is very *different from* glass.<br><br>New York differs from Chicago in that it has more pollution and more restaurants. |

## 8) Compare with/Compare to

| **Compare with** (For *differences* between people or things) | My style of writing cannot be *compared with* his style of writing. |
|---|---|
| **Compare to** (For similarities) | Nike's new Air Jordan shoe is *comparable to* its past versions; they both look very similar. |

## 9) Succeed In / Succeeded at (Both OK)

| Succeed in : This is used when talking about succeeding in a certain position or task | I hope that I will succeed in finishing my report on time. |
|---|---|
| Succeed at:  This can also be used when it relates to a task. | It was Joe Torre who finally *succeeded at* bringing the Yankees back to the World Series. |

## 10)  Mistrust of

| Mistrust of | He is mistrustful of people who don't speak much. |
|---|---|

## 11)  In the Hope of or  In the Hopes of (In the hopes to)

### *Example Sentence:*

The zoo submitted proposals to several non-profit foundations *in the hopes of* gaining money for its new aquarium.

## 12) Condemn as (Not condemn to be)

The reality show, *Keeping Up with the Kardashians*, has been ***condemned as*** vacuous.

....................................................................

# More on idioms

*Below are some common mistakes made with idioms. Corrections are in parentheses.*

1. .They <u>so</u> complicated the process <u>as</u> to ruin its efficiency. (should be ***that*** ... its efficiency was ruined.)

2. <u>No sooner</u> had he gone to work <u>but</u> his boss told him not to. (should be ***than***)

3. Lawyers representing the salesman <u>asserted</u> <u>as to</u> the defensibility of his practices. (should be ***that*** ... his practices could be defended.)

4. We have the power to <u>determine</u> <u>if</u> he'll be hired. (should be ***whether***)

<u>Just as</u> John has chosen physics <u>and</u> his brother chosen science-related field. (should ***so has***)

6. The <u>reason</u> she passed was <u>because</u> she studied all night. (should be **that**)
{"Because" is used when "reason" is **not**, as in "She passed *because* she studied all night."}

7. Mr. John Smith <u>arrived to</u> New York last evening. (should be **in**)

8. All of the survivors refused <u>offers for</u> assistance. (should be **of**)

9. <u>The number</u> of people absent today <u>are</u> surprising. (should be **is**) {"A number" goes with the plural "are," "were," or plural action verb such as "<u>A</u> number of people <u>escape</u> to the mountains each summer for vacation.}

10. Infants become more <u>capable to</u> distinguish various symbols... (should be **of** distinguish<u>ing</u> ...)

11. That company has been helping families since 1977, <u>annually</u> distributing food to hundreds of families <u>each year</u>. ("each year" is not needed since it is redundant)

12. That corral reef is the only one of <u>a</u> kind. (should be **its**)

13. That teacher seems to have a <u>preoccupation on</u> word problems. (should be **with**)

. Generic drugs are not nearly <u>as</u> expensive to purchase <u>than</u> name brands. (should
*as*)

. Background in that field is not a condition <u>necessary in</u> the understanding of the
ɔcess. (should be *for*)

. Malaria is still a <u>threat of</u> travelers in foreign countries. (should be *to*)

. The exchange between teacher and student promotes learning far different from
at <u>which results as</u> the student listens but does not participate. (should be *if*)

. Debs Garms is <u>regarded to be</u> the batting leader with the fewest at bats in a
ason. (should be *as*)

. Most people <u>prefer</u> the mall <u>more than</u> downtown stores. (should be *to*)

. The coach vehemently <u>protested over</u> that foul the referee called. ("over" is
ɹundant)

. Many players, if given the chance to relive the moment, would choose <u>to do it</u>.
ɹould be *so*)

22. It's difficult for a doctor to <u>choose between</u> engaging in private practice <u>or</u> engaging in research. (should be ***and***) {"You can ***choose*** red ***or*** blue"  ***but***... "You can ***choose <u>between</u>*** red ***and*** blue."

23. <u>Far away</u> from being a diehard fan, he had only a passing interest. ("away" is redundant)

24. The jurors quickly perceived his statements were <u>inconsistent to</u> those made earlier. (should be ***with***)

25. In a <u>world that</u> the rate of change is so rapid, it's hard to keep up at times. (should be ***where***)

26. She was <u>listening at</u> that song so intently, I could not get her attention. (should be ***to***)

\*\*\*\*\*\*\*\*\*\*\*\*\*\*\*\*\*\*\*\*\*\*\*\*\*\*\*\*\*\*\*\*\*\*\*\*\*\*\*\*\*\*\*\*\*\*\*\*\*\*\*\*\*\*\*\*\*\*\*\*\*\*\*\*\*\*\*\*\*\*\*\*\*\*\*\*\*\*\*\*\*\*
\*\*\*\*\*\*\*

## MORE IDIOM WORK

If you want to crack 700 and/or get the highest score you can,  knowing the idiomatic rules below is imperative. Here are most of them in brief:

complicated everything ...... *that*...          *asserted that*...          *no sooner* had he ..... *than* ...

*termine whether*...          *just as* he ..... *so* has she...    *reason* he passed was *that* ...

*arrived in*...          refused *offers of* ...          *a* number *are*/ *the number is* ...

*apable of* distinguishing ...          **only one** of *its* kind...          **preoccupation** *with*...

not nearly *as* expensive *as* ...          not *necessary for*...          a *threat to* travelers...

*egarded as* the most talented...          *prefer* the car *to* the train... choose *to do so*...

choose *between* red *and* blue...          remarks *inconsistent with*...          *listening to* the song...

in a ***world*** *<u>where</u>* change is so rapid...          <u>Three Redundancies</u>: Take trips annually (each year)...,

He protested (over) that foul..., and          Far (away) from being a diehard fan ...[delete words in (x)]

# NEW IDIOMS YOU LEARN

As you learned from Mr. Buffer's SAT/ACT Program, idioms are rules of language that are irregular in their usage. As you come across new ones in your learning, and get clarification on them, write them below and study them frequently.

# FOUNDATIONAL CONCEPT#3:

# Less Vs. fewer

**Example#1:** Is this sentence correct?

*The cookie jar has less cookies than it did yesterday.*

**Answer:** *No! This sentence is incorrect?* Why? The reason is that when a subject can be measured or broken down into numerical or individual units, you should use the word **"fewer, "** not the word **"less."** When something cannot be divided into individual units, you would use the word *"less. "*

For example, you cannot have *fewer light* in the room. You would say: "When I closed the drapes, there was *less* light coming in." It would not make sense to say: "When I closed the drapes, there was **fewer** light coming in."

But, you can say: "There were *fewer rays of light* coming in." Why? Because rays of light can be broken down into individual units!

## Less Vs. fewer (Continued)

**************************

## Part 2:  Practice:

(Try these examples): Are these correct? Why or why not?  If it is written correctly, circle "Correct." If the sentence is written incorrectly, circle "Incorrect", and rewrite the sentence correctly on the line below.

1) John has *less* coins than his brother does.

(CORRECT/INCORRECT)

_____

_____ .


2) John has *fewer* love for school this year than he had last year.

(CORRECT/INCORRECT)

_____ .


3) Raina has *fewer* shirts in her closet this year compared to how many she had last year.

(CORRECT/INCORRECT)

_____ .


## PART 3: YOUR TURN

1) Write a sentence correctly using the word "less."

_____ .


2)   Write a sentence correctly using the word "fewer."

_____ .

# FOUNDATIONAL CONCEPT#4: TRANSITIONS

## Lesson Notes:   Why are transitions important?

## (Read with student)

Transitions are important to help create a flow between paragraphs and act as a bridge between sentences and paragraphs.    They also help to keep the reader's attention.   Understanding transitions better will help you understand what the SAT and ACT is looking for when they ask you to decipher good writing flow and effective Unity and Coherence.

# If you want to......

## A) Add Information to your Writing:

Again
Besides
Moreover
And
Likewise
Similarly
Furthermore
Additionally
Also
For example

> **Usage example:**
> George Washington was more than just our first President. He was also a great war general. Additionally, he was the President of the Constitutional Convention, and many feel that he is the main reason why the U. S. Constitution was ratified.

## B) Conclude or Summarize an idea, paragraph, or essay

Finally
In summary
In short
In conclusion
Consequently
All in all
As a result
To sum up
Summing up
Therefore
Thus
To conclude

> **Usage example:**
> Therefore, one can see based on the evidence in this essay that Abraham Lincoln was a truly great President and saved the union...

## If you want to......

## C)   Contrast two things or show a difference:

but
otherwise
conversely
even so
yet
however
counter to
on the other hand
as opposed to
on the contrary
nevertheless
still

<u>Usage example:</u>
1) Mrs. Balter knew that her two sons couldn't be more different.   Darren was an athlete and liked to go to baseball games with his friends. **On the other hand**, Jake liked to stay home and read and play video games.

## D)   Emphasize a point:

Again
Indeed
To repeat
Truly
In fact
To emphasize

<u>Usage example:</u>
Thomas Jefferson was said to be one of the smartest American leaders in history. **In fact**, President Kennedy once said to a group of smart college presidents at the White House "This is most intellect in one room in the White House since Thomas Jefferson dined alone."

For this reason
With this in mind

E)  **<u>Practice</u>**

**<u>Directions:</u>**  Write 2 paragraphs or 8 total sentences using some of the transitions you learned.

_____

_____

_____

_____

_____

_____

_____

_____

_____

_____

_____

_____

_____

_____

# FOUNDATIONAL CONCEPT#5
# UNDERSTANDING IRREGULAR VERBS

## IMPORTANT PRINCIPLES AND STUDY DIRECTIVES

**#1:** A regular verb in its regular past form ends with the letters "ed." For example, the verb *bark* (a regular verb) used in its simple past form would be used as *barked*. Some verbs, though, are *irregular* and formed in a way other than adding "ed" to them. Some of these ending forms have to be memorized because there is no consistent and perfect pattern to their formation.

**#2:** Two forms of a verb we are going to study as part of this lesson are the "simple past" form and the "past participle" form. Past participle verb forms come after the words "has", "had", or "have."

**#3:** As you will see when we go over these with you, these verbs form 5 distinct groups.

**#4:**   You should study these as part of your weekly study plan.  Knowing these verb endings can be the difference between 4-6 questions on the SAT, thus resulting in a possible 70-100-point swing.

### Here is an example of a question in which knowledge of irregular verb endings factors in:

1)   John is convinced that because <u>sea levels have rose</u> so high it is virtually impossible to deny the reality of global warming.

    A)   sea levels have rose
    B)   sea levels would rise
    C)   sea levels have risen
    D)   sea levels had rose
    E)   sea levels were to rise

    The correct answer is answer choice "C."  In order to know this for sure, though, you have to know that "risen" is the past participle form of the verb rise.

# LESSON AND STUDY

*Now, let's turn to page 130-132 of your Blue, Language Network textbook and learn about the different past participle forms. These should be studied regularly!*

# Mr. Buffer's SAT/ACT
## ScoreMax Program

## OTHER VITAL SAT/ACT LANGUAGE/WRITING STRATEGY NOTES FROM MR. BUFFER OR MY CAMBRIDGE  TEACHERS

**Date**_____

_____
_____
_____
_____
_____
_____
_____
_____
_____.

**Date**_____

_____

_____

_____

_____

_____

_____

_____

_____

_____.

**Date**_____

_____

_____

_____

_____

_____

_____

_____

_____

_____.

**Date**_____

_____

_____

_____

_____

_____

_____

_____

_____

_____.

**Date**_____

_____

_____

_____

_____

_____

_____

_____

_____.

**Date**_____

_____

_____

_____

_____

_____

_____

_____

_____

_____.

**Date**_____

_____

_____

_____

_____

_____

_____

_____

_____

_____.

49

**Date**_____

_____
_____
_____
_____
_____
_____
_____
_____
_____•

**Date**_____

_____
_____
_____
_____
_____
_____
_____
_____•

# JOURNAL PART II:

# MASTERING THE SAT-ACT

# EVIDENCED-BASED

# READING SECTION

**The following interview was done with Mr. Buffer by a trained interviewer and his responses are transcribed below. Your teacher will read through his answers with you prior to going over the Reading strategies.**

\*\*\*\*\*\*\*\*\*\*\*\*\*\*\*\*\*\*\*\*\*\*\*\*\*\*\*\*\*\*\*\*\*\*\*\*\*\*\*\*\*\*

1) **Question for Mr. Buffer:** Mr. Buffer, what is the key to mastering the Reading sections of the SAT and ACT?

**Answer from Mr. Buffer:**   The key to mastering the section is to remember that you are not reading this passage to understand it for the long-term as you do in school.   You should be primarily focused on reading the passage to correctly answer the questions. While this might sound on the one hand basic, and on the other hand contradictory to what we as classroom (Mr. Buffer was a secondary classroom teacher for over a decade in the public schools) teachers are telling our students every day, it is nonetheless vital that students fully grasp this.  It is also, of course, more important for students to read a variety of different material, even outside their standard high school coursework, and to have a robust and varied vocabulary, skills and practices we encourage, foster and help with here at Cambridge Learning Center of New Jersey in North Brunswick.

2) **Question for Mr. Buffer:**  What have been some of the biggest success stories you have seen at Cambridge Learning Center concerning Evidence-Based Reading that you like to tell?

   **Answer from Mr. Buffer**:     We have had so many students get 750 + on the Reading/Writing section. The best stories I like to tell are when students finally grasp the idea that they are to become very evidenced-based readers, not creative readers. When students go to college and even to graduate school, which most of our students are going to do, they are going to be required to read sophisticated material, some with complex opinions and perspectives in them. It is essential that students can learn and understand this content with an open mind and not insert their own opinion while reading.  Doing so can interfere with the clarity needed to grasp the author's point of view.
   There have been significant thinkers throughout history whose wisdom has been passed down through the ages: Kant, Jefferson, Voltaire, Kierkegaard, and more. Whether students agree or disagree with their opinions, they should be able to read them and understand what they are expressing without inserting our own ideas.  This is what

the Evidence-Based reading section is asking us to do: to be able to read something and clearly see what's on the page, regardless of what we think about it.

To be able to see the evidence presented in a reading, a newspaper article, or a book excerpt clearly and openly, without any of our own filters or biases is an essential skill. It has been a great pleasure for me to see students have their scores jump from 650 to 750 who have finally grasped this concept and get on a path to seeing their dreams come true.

# The New York Times

## A GREAT TOOL TO HELP YOU ENRICH YOU'RE READING SKILLS AND PERFORM BETTER ON THE SAT/ACT

*\* To help you with your reading comprehension, breadth of knowledge, and exposure to sophisticated levels of writing, as well as different writing styles, **you should make a goal each week to read a minimum of 4 full editorials from the New York Times Opinion Page or articles from any other section of the New York Times.***

*\* Circle any vocabulary words you don't know **and define them in the Vocabulary Section of this workbook.***

## The websites to find the articles and editorials are:

## www.nytimes.com

## Www.nytimes.com/opinion

# MR. BUFFER'S  WEEKLY

## SAT STUDY PLAN AND  BEST PRACTICES FOR YOUR OPTIMAL SCORE: UPDATED 8/19/16

A) Study your SAT flashcards daily for all areas- Reading, Writing, and Math.  Try to average 40 new cards per week, and make this process cumulative.  Also, make sure you are taking *Mr. Buffer's Online SAT Vocabulary Test* bi-weekly as this will greatly help you with the Critical Reading section of the test.

***B)***   Aim to review your mistakes from in-class and from your previously checked homework from all SAT/ACT Subject Areas (Math, Reading, and Writing). You should be taking notes during your sessions and studying them at home.   This is how most of your time should be spent.  ***Before taking practice test after practice test, and asking to take test after test, you should focus on studying.***  What I (Mr. Buffer) have always told students is that *"**You don't test your way to success.  You study your way to success."**   **This should be done for 1.5 hours per day minimum, but you should aim for more.***

C) Come to class ready to ask questions to your teachers, and you can also ask Mr. Buffer any questions you have about SAT prep.   You can also see or make an appointment with Mr. Buffer (Cambridge Founder and Owner) at any time about questions related to college choice. Just make an appointment with the front desk.

D) We will automatically book you for a progress test every 24 hours of SAT Tutoring. Make sure you are checking your e-mail for these notifications; you can also ask at the front desk for your testing schedule. If you cannot come in for your test, it will be your job to contact us to reschedule.

E) Your homework will mostly be supplemental work. You do not have to time yourself for this. This is your time to refine your skills.

F) **Practice tests at home:** Sometimes for homework you can time yourself and take a practice test, but this is separate from your Cambridge homework, but make sure someone else times you. You should make things as close to real testing conditions as possible.

G) Keep yourself motivated by trying to get a little better each day, not expecting huge leaps in one day or one week. Success is built one moment at a time! We are here to help you succeed!

SUCCESS

\* \* \* \* \* \* \* \* \* \* \* \* \* \* \* \* \*

## MR. BUFFER'S  WEEKLY

## ACT STUDY PLAN AND  BEST PRACTICES FOR YOUR OPTIMAL SCORE

9)  Study your ACT flashcards daily *for all areas- Reading, Writing, Math, and Science.* Try to average 30-40 new cards per week, and make this process cumulative.  Also, make sure you are taking *Mr. Buffer's Online SAT/ACT Vocabulary Test* bi-weekly as this will greatly help you with the Reading section of the test, and help make sure your vocabulary is strong to be integrated into your ACT Essay.

*10)*       Aim to review your mistakes from in-class and from your previously checked homework from all ACT Subject Areas (Math, Reading, Science, and Writing). You should be taking notes during your sessions and studying them at home. This is how most of your time should be spent. *Before taking practice test after practice test, and/or asking to take test after test, you should focus on studying.* What I (Mr. Buffer) have always told students is that *"You don't test your way to success. You study your way to success." This should be done for 1.5 hours per day minimum, but you should aim for more.*

11)     Come to class ready to ask questions to your teachers, and you can also ask Mr. Buffer any questions you have about ACT prep. You can also see or make an appointment with Mr. Buffer (Cambridge Founder and Owner) at any time about questions related to college choice. Just make an appointment with the front desk

12)     We will automatically book you for a progress test every 24 hours of ACT Tutoring. You can also ask at the front desk for your testing schedule. If you cannot come in for your test, it will be your job to contact us to reschedule.

13)     Study all of your other SA Sheets (These are for ACT). These will help you maximally prepare for the ACT.

14)    Be regularly aware of your major areas for growth and make sure your Live Work Journal is always being signed.


15)    You will do a lot of ACT problems for homework. Make sure that you are jotting down notes you have to bring in with your teachers.

16)    Here is what a typical day can look like for ACT studying:

   A) 40-65 Minutes: Homework ACT Problems (Assigned)

   B) 40-65 Minutes:  Review and Study previous mistakes, flashcards (See procedure and details above), and write down questions I have to bring into class.


9) Your homework will mostly be supplemental work.  You do not have to time yourself for this.  This is your time to refine your skills.


12)**Practice tests at home:** Sometimes for homework you can time yourself and take a practice test, but this is separate from your Cambridge homework, but make sure someone else times you when you do.  You should make things as close to real testing conditions as possible.

**13)** Keep yourself motivated by trying to get a little better each day, not expecting huge leaps in one day or one week. Success is built one moment at a time! We are here to help you succeed!

# Mr. Buffer's SAT/ACT
## ScoreMax Program

\*\*\*\*\*\*\*\*\*\*\*\*\*\*\*\*\*\*\*\*\*\*\*\*

# *BEST PRACTICES FOR STUDENTS*

## More SAT Study Tips and Best Practices

1)	Each week, for at least 10.5 hours per week (an average of 1.5 hours per day), review your notes from your in-class Live Work and homework check mistakes.   Do this for all of your subject areas of your SAT and/or ACT program.   This is a key component of your improvement.   As the Cambridge SAT/ACT Success Plan Pie Chart expresses, you cannot just count on your sessions here to reach your optimal score! You deserve the best and only the best for yourself and for your future; therefore, an average of one hour per day, in addition to your homework, is well worth a brighter future!

2) Try your best not to miss sessions. Do your best to arrange your schedule so that you can attend your sessions and be on time. Our data show that students who attend class consistently, and don't miss class have the highest score improvements!

3) If you don't understand something, ask your teacher! We are here to help! Do not hesitate in this area and hold back.

4) If you have a question about your program, your academic future as it relates to school or the SAT, or any other matter that relates to your overall education plan, please make an appointment at the front desk to meet with Mr. Buffer.

5) Remember to get out of what Mr. Buffer and team call *"school-mode"* when preparing for and taking your SAT/ACT. Your examinations and assessments in school are designed by teachers who know their students well and are usually not designed with an intent to tempt you to make wrong answer choices. Standardized tests such as the SAT and ACT, on the other hand, are often designed with answer choices that can "throw you off" and truly and quite bluntly are there to trick you. Part of preparing for the SAT/ACT is learning to recognize these attempts, thus making you a better test-taker.

# OUR HIGHLY-PROVEN

# SAT& ACT EVIDENCE-BASED READING STRATEGIES

*BOTH TESTS' CONTENT WILL BE COVERED IN THE DISCUSSIONS BELOW*

**Tip#1:** **Look for Key Words in the passages that serves as guideposts towards the correct answer**

## SAT:

Remember to always look for key words in the passages as you answer the questions. These will help guide you to the correct answer. There must be a direct link between the answer choice you choose and words in the passage. *There is no reading between the lines; only what is on the lines.* You should think of the key words as clues left for you on a trail on the way to a treasure: Like the clues, they will guide you to the correct answer. Your teacher will help you understand this concept more in depth as you do practice questions, live work, and homework review, and it will be vital for you to take notes.

**ACT:** There are also key words on this test that the test designer has to provide to make the answer choices fit for a standardized test that your teacher has been trained to help you find. So, rest assured you will learn how to do this well.

## Tip#2: Distinguish between Fact and Opinion

**SAT:** When you are reading non-fiction passages, be sure to quickly and consistently differentiate, in your mind, between what the passage is stating as a fact and what the author is stating as his or her opinion. This will help you with your comprehension because you will learn to discern context and tone better. Your teacher will help you with this and has been trained by me (Mr. Buffer) to help you answer questions better and quicker on this. The test makers have made this process easier than you think and we will help you with this more and more as you spend more time with us.

**ACT: The ACT Reading section has 4 different kinds of readings and 3 of them are almost always non-fiction, so this strategy is very applicable. It will be very important that as you are reading, you learn to recognize a shift in tone away from fact and towards opinion. We will teach you this and as with the SAT your teachers have been well trained in how to do this.**

## Tip#3:  Don't spend too much time on 1 question!

**SAT/ACT**:  This goes for both tests!  You don't have much time to spare, so don't let your ego get the best of you.  If you don't know a question, leave it blank and move on!   All the items are worth the same value!!  This is so important to keep in mind.

## Tip#4:  Read the passages as literally as possible without inserting your own opinion

**SAT/ACT:**  It can be tempting when reading the SAT/ACT passages to want to give your own opinion or to comment on the stories.   You are not reading for this purpose though.   Your job is to understand the author's perspective, not your own perspective, as best as possible

## Tip#5:  Use the "Cambridge SAT/ACT Time Efficiency Reading Strategy" © ™ for longer passages and for Comparative Passages:

**SAT/ACT:**  For the passages that make up the 52-question Evidenced-Based Reading section, we will train you to do the Line Questions first!   The purpose of this strategy is to enable you to save time and to mitigate your anxiety.   Your SAT/ACT teacher will explain to you how to do this in more detail.  By the time you have finished all of your line questions, you should be able to answer the other questions more efficiently.  With practice, you will get the hang of this!  We will show you how to do this with mastery.

## Tip# 6: Avoid very extreme or absolute words

**SAT/ACT:**  One of the most evident indicators of poor choices is those words that make a statement extreme or absolute.   As you learned in Cambridge Evidenced-Based Reading Tip#4, you have to take every word literally. If you do, you'll realize that specific answer choices that seem plausible, or in accord with the overall theme of the passage, are actually poor choices. For example, take a look at the following sentences:

- You should always eat right before going to school.

- All babies should play as much as possible as exercise is good for cognitive development.

While these two sentences are examples of how we speak in daily conversations, they make for poor choices on the SAT because, when taken literally, they mean very different things than what is actually intended.  Words such as "always", "never", and "all" are very strong words in the context of the SAT and are rarely contained within the correct answer choice.

Some other words and phrases that often indicate extreme answers that are rarely the correct choices are:

-All, always, the only, oldest, the first, same.

-superlatives (such as best, biggest, greatest)

-and "less" words (such as pointless, useless, endless)

All of the words above often suggest sweeping generalizations that are often too extreme. Correct answers for the Critical Reading Passages are usually presented in more moderate terms such as:

-Not all, not always, seemed the only, oldest known, among the first, about the same

*Keep in mind that there are no foolproof rules on extreme words. These are just some of the words that often – but not always – indicate good or bad choices. What's more important is the principle underlying them. Always remember to keep context in mind.

Here they are listed side-by-side so that you can more clearly see the differences:

| Indicators of Extreme Answers (poor choices) | More Moderate Versions (better choices) |
|---|---|
| All | not all |
| always | not always |
| the only | seemed the only |
| oldest | oldest known |
| the first | among the first |

| same | about the same |
|------|----------------|

### Tip#7 Avoid choices that defy common sense

**SAT/ACT:** The concept above to "use common sense" may seem obvious, but it's easy to get caught up in the details of the passages that you overlook these. In each set of answer choices, there will sometimes be at least one answer choice that you know is so ridiculous that it most certainly cannot be the answer. Your intuition is correct. You should certainly avoid these options.

### Tip#8:

**SAT/ACT** : Avoid choices that require you to infer beyond the limits of the passage

This ties in with some of the other strategies. There is something called "inference" questions on the Evidence-Based Reading passages, but they're not what you think. Many students mistake the SAT's asking them to infer as an opportunity to assume something beyond the limits of the passage. DO NOT! These questions are not asking you to guess or jump to some conclusion; DO NOT read into things. These questions simply require you to look into specific parts of the passage and find the answers. If you find yourself thinking up a hypothetical question in your head to justify an answer, it's probably the wrong choice.

Remember that this is a standardized test. The answer must be something that most other students can "infer" from the passage, not something random you draw up in your head.

Just to reiterate this point, let us look at the directions at the top of every Evidence-Based Reading Section of the SAT:

Each passage or pair of passages below is followed by several questions. Read each passage or pair and then choose the best answer to each question based on what is stated or implied in the passage or passages and in any accompanying graphics (such as a table or graph). Tip#9: Look to eliminate wrong answers first!

## Tip#9: Use Process of Elimination

**SAT/ACT** : Don't be so quick to want to answer the questions with the first answer choice you think is correct. You should get into the habit of *eliminating wrong answers first.* Your SAT/ACT teacher will help you with this and aid you in understanding why Process of Elimination is so essential.

## Tip#10: Remember that there is no substitute for regular reading and study

**SAT/ACT** : These tips are not meant to be a panacea: they are simply some tips to help you do better on the Evidence-Based Reading section. There is no better way to prepare for the SAT, the ACT, for college, and for life than to read as much as you can and to study as much vocabulary as you can!!

vocab in context questions:

1. Think of own one word defintion

2. Substitute each answer choice for the word

# VOCABULARY LEARNING SECTION

## NEW SAT/ACT VOCABULARY ADDITIONAL WORDS
## I WILL DEFINE AND LEARN

1. **Word:** audacious
   **Definition:** adj.
   daring, bold
   _____
   _____ .

2. **Word:** prognosticate verb
   **Definition:**
   an event in the future
   to foretell
   _____ .

**3. Word:** tempest
   **Definition:**
   a violent windy storm
                                                    .

**4. Word:** ebullience
   **Definition:**
   quality of being cheerful
                                                    .

**5. Word:** disconsolation
   **Definition:**
   not given sorrow or pity
                                                    .

**6. Word:** dirge
   **Definition:**
   a lament for the dead
                                                    .

**7. Word:** menial

**Definition:**

not requiring much skill
and lacking prestige
.

8. **Word:** convulsed
   **Definition:**

   sudden violent irregular
   movements of the body
   caused by involuntary contraction

9. **Word:** indulgent
   **Definition:**

   having a tendency to be overly
   generous to or lenient with
   someone
   .

10. **Word:** timorous
    **Definition:**

    showing or suffering from
    nervousness, fear or lack
    of confidence
    .

**11. Word:** desolate

  **Definition:**

deserted of people

                                                          .

**12. Word:** torpid

  **Definition:**

mentally or physically inactive

                                                           .

**13. Word:** assiduous

  **Definition:**

showing great care or perseverance

                                                           .

**14. Word:** vessel

  **Definition:**

a duct or canal containing blood or other fluid; ship; a person

**15. Word:** muzzled

**Definition:**

prevent from doing something
ex/ dog bark

                                                .

16. **Word:** encapsulate
   **Definition:**

   express features distinctly

                                                .

17. **Word:** bipartisanship
   **Definition:**

   involving the agreement or
   cooperation of two
   political parties            .

18. **Word:** subsequent
   **Definition:**

   later, happening after

                                                .

19. Word: *philology* nonphilological

 Definition:
 branch of knowledge that
 deals w/ structure, relationships
 of a language                    .

20. Word: introspective

 Definition:
 self-analyzing
 observation of own's mental
 and emotional process            .

21. Word: scarcely

 Definition:

 _____

 _____

 _____.

22. Word: *ubiquitous* pervasive

 Definition:
 Spreading widely
 throughout an area or
 group                            .

23. Word: _____

**Definition:**

_____

_____

_____.

**24. Word:** radical

  **Definition:**

profound; change relating to
fundamental nature

_____.

**25. Word:** _____

  **Definition:**

_____

_____

_____.

**26. Word:** _____

  **Definition:**

_____

_____

_____.

**27. Word:** _____

**Definition:**

_____

_____

_____ .


**28. Word:** _____
 **Definition:**

_____

_____

_____ .


**29. Word:** _____
 **Definition:**

_____

_____

_____ .


**30. Word:** _____
 **Definition:**

_____

_____

_____ .


**31. Word:** _____

**Definition:**

_____

_____

_____.

**32. Word:** _____
  **Definition:**

_____

_____

_____.

**33. Word:** _____
  **Definition:**

_____

_____

_____.

**34. Word:** _____
  **Definition:**

_____

_____

_____.

**35. Word:** _____

**Definition:**

_____

_____

_____.

**36. Word:** _____
  **Definition:**

_____

_____

_____.

**37. Word:** _____
  **Definition:**

_____

_____

_____.

**38. Word:** _____
  **Definition:**

_____

_____

_____.

**39. Word:** _____

**Definition:**

_____

_____

_____.

**40. Word:** _____
  **Definition:**

_____

_____

_____.

**41. Word:** _____
  **Definition:**

_____

_____

_____.

**42. Word:** _____
  **Definition:**

_____

_____

_____.

**43. Word:** _____

Definition:

_____

_____

_____.

44. Word: _____
   Definition:

_____

_____

_____.

45. Word: _____
   Definition:

_____

_____

_____.

46. Word: _____
   Definition:

_____

_____

_____.

47. Word: _____

**Definition:**

_____

_____

_____.

**48.Word:** _____
   **Definition:**

_____

_____

_____.

**49.Word:** _____
   **Definition:**

_____

_____

_____.

**50.** Word: _____

   Definition:

_____

_____

_____.

**51.** Word: _____

   Definition:

_____

_____

_____.

**52.** Word: _____

   Definition:

_____

_____

_____.

**53.** Word: _____

   Definition:

_____

_____

_____.

**54. Word:** _____

   **Definition:**

   _____

   _____

   _____.

**55. Word:** _____

   **Definition:**

   _____

   _____

   _____.

**56. Word:** _____

   **Definition:**

   _____

   _____

   _____.

57. Word: _____

  Definition:

_____

_____

_____ .


58. Word: _____

  Definition:

_____

_____

_____ .


59. Word: _____

  Definition:

_____

_____

_____ .

**60.Word:** _____

  **Definition:**

_____

_____

_____.


**61.Word:** _____

  **Definition:**

_____

_____

_____.

**62. Word:** _____

   **Definition:** _____

_____

_____

_____ .


**63. Word:** _____

   **Definition:** _____

_____

_____

_____ .


**64. Word:** _____

   **Definition:** _____

_____

_____

_____ .

**65. Word:** _____

  **Definition:**

_____

_____

_____.


**66. Word:** _____

  **Definition:**

_____

_____

_____.


**67. Word:** _____

  **Definition:**

_____

_____

_____.

**68. Word:** _____

   **Definition:**

_____

_____

_____.


**69. Word:** _____

   **Definition:**

_____

_____

_____.


**70. Word:** _____

   **Definition:**

_____

_____

_____.

71. Word: _____

   Definition:

_____

_____

_____.

72. Word: _____

   Definition:

_____

_____

_____.

73. Word: _____

   Definition:

_____

_____

_____.

**74. Word:** _____
   **Definition:**

_____

_____

_____.

**75. Word:** _____
   **Definition:**

_____

_____

_____.

**76. Word:** _____
   **Definition:**

_____

_____

_____.

**77. Word:** _____

 **Definition:**

_____

_____

_____.

**78. Word:** _____

 **Definition:**

_____

_____

_____.

**79. Word:** _____

 **Definition:**

_____

_____

_____.

**80. Word:** _____

 **Definition:**

_____

_____

_____.

**81. Word:** _____

  **Definition:**

  _____

  _____

  _____ .


**82. Word:** _____

  **Definition:**

  _____

  _____

  _____ .


**83. Word:** _____

  **Definition:**

  _____

  _____

  _____ .


**84. Word:** _____

  **Definition:**

  _____

  _____

  _____ .


**85. Word:** _____

**Definition:**

_____

_____

_____.

**86. Word:** _____
   **Definition:**

_____

_____

_____.

**87. Word:** _____
   **Definition:**

_____

_____

_____.

**88. Word:** _____

  **Definition:** _____

_____

_____

_____.

**89. Word:** _____

  **Definition:** _____

_____

_____

_____.

**90. Word:** _____

  **Definition:** _____

_____

_____

_____.

**91. Word:** _____

   **Definition:**

_____

_____

_____.

**92. Word:** _____

   **Definition:**

_____

_____

_____.

**93. Word:** _____

   **Definition:**

_____

_____

_____.

**94. Word:** _____
   **Definition:**

   _____

   _____

   _____.

**95. Word:** _____
   **Definition:**

   _____

   _____

   _____.

**96. Word:** _____
   **Definition:**

   _____

   _____

   _____.

**97.    Word:** _____
   **Definition:**

   _____

   _____

   _____.

**98. Word:** _____

   **Definition:**

_____

_____

_____ .

**99. Word:** _____

   **Definition:**

_____

_____

_____ .

**100.   Word:** _____

   **Definition:**

_____

_____

_____ .

**101.   Word:** _____

   **Definition:**

_____

_____

_____ .

**102.   Word:** _____

**Definition:**

_____

_____

_____.

**103.** **Word:**_____

  **Definition:**

_____

_____

_____.

Mr. Buffer's SAT/ACT

ScoreMax Program

# OTHER VITAL READING STRATEGY NOTES FROM MR. BUFFER OR MY CAMBRIDGE READING TEACHERS

**Date** _____

_____

_____

_____

_____

_____

_____

_____

_____

_____.

**Date** _____

_____

_____

_____

_____

_____

_____

_____

_____

_____.

**Date**_____


_____
_____
_____
_____
_____
_____
_____

_____.

**Date**_____


_____
_____
_____
_____
_____
_____
_____

_____.

**Date**_____

_____

_____

_____

_____

_____

_____

_____

_____

_____.

**Date**_____

_____

_____

_____

_____

_____

_____

_____

_____.

**Date**_____

_____

_____

_____
_____
_____
_____
_____
_____
_____.

**Date**_____

_____
_____
_____
_____
_____
_____
_____.

**Date**_____

_____
_____
_____
_____
_____

_____

_____

_____

_____.

**Date**_____

_____

_____

_____

_____

_____

_____

_____

_____.

**Date**_____

_____

_____

_____

_____

_____

_____

_____

_____
_____.

**Date**_____

_____
_____
_____
_____
_____
_____
_____
_____
_____.

**Date**_____

_____
_____
_____
_____
_____
_____
_____
_____.

**Date**_____

_____
_____
_____
_____
_____
_____
_____
_____
_____.

**Date**_____

_____
_____
_____
_____
_____
_____
_____
_____
_____.

**Date**_____

_____
_____
_____
_____
_____
_____
_____
_____
_____.

**Date**_____

_____
_____
_____
_____
_____
_____
_____
_____
_____.

**Date**_____

_____
_____
_____

_____

_____

_____

_____

_____

_____.

**Date**_____

_____

_____

_____

_____

_____

_____

_____

_____

_____.

**Date**_____

_____

_____

_____

_____

Made in the USA
Columbia, SC
13 March 2018